DON'T BUMP THE GLUMP!

and Other Fantasies

DON'T BUMP THE GLUMP!

and Other Fantasies

by
Shel Silverstein

HarperCollins*Publishers*

ISBN-13: 978-0-545-11072-3
ISBN-10: 0-545-11072-6

Uncle Shelby's Zoo: Don't Bump the Glump! and Other Fantasies
Copyright © 1964, renewed 1992 Evil Eye, LLC
Most of the material in this book originally appeared in *Playboy Magazine* and
is reprinted with permission. © 1960, 1962, 1963, HMH Publishing Co., Inc.

12 11 10 9 8 7 6 5 4 3 2 1   8 9 10 11 12 13/0

Printed in Mexico   49

First Scholastic printing, September 2008

For Peggy

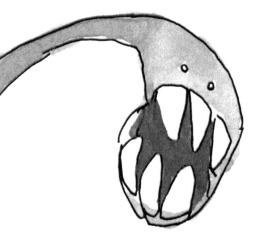

PROLOGUE

Now the Bears and the Bees and the Chinpanazees
Are creatures with which we're familiar.
But what do we know of the Humplebacked Mo,
Or the Ring-Tailed Breckspeckled Hillyar?
Or the Tongue-Twisted Rubber-Necked Bylliar?
Or the Gorp-Eating Kallikozilliar?

GLUMP

A WARNING FOR THOSE WHO CHANCE TO
MEET A WILD GLUMP COMING HOME LATE
AT NIGHT, DOWN A DARK STREET, PAST
A GRAVEYARD, ALL ALONE IN A STORM

DON'T BUMP
THE GLUMP.

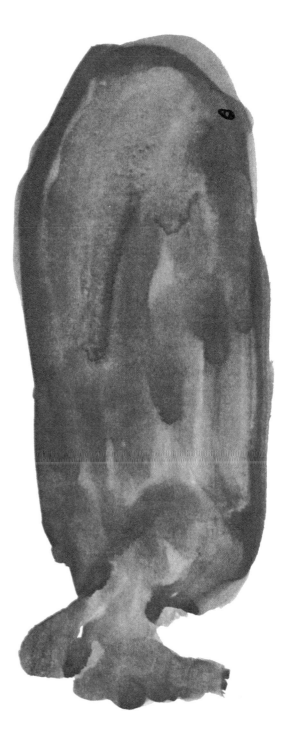

QUICK-DISGUISING GINNIT

This is the Quick-Disguising Ginnit.
Didn't he have you fooled for a minute?

THE ACCIDENT

I think I've killed a Dickeree.
I did it by mistake.
I thought she was a ball,
So I bounced her off the wall;
I had no idea at all
That she might break.

THE CRAWFEE

That silly fish, the Crawfee,
Has been swimming in my coffee.
But now I've drunk it up
And he isn't in the cup.
And he's nowhere to be found. . . .
Do you think that he has drowned?

UNDERSLUNG ZATH

I fear the wrath
Of the Underslung Zath.
Will someone else tell him
It's time for his bath?

ZRBANGDRALDNK

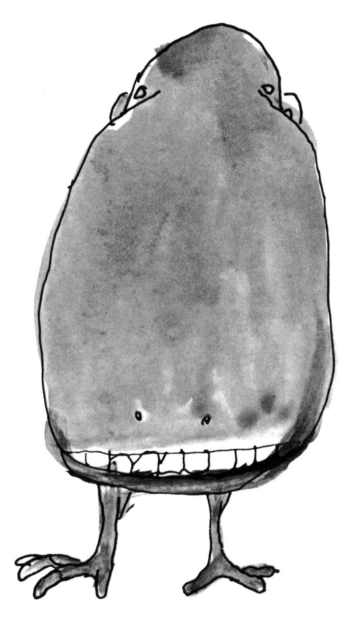

The Zrbangdraldnk has just arrived
And it's up to me to announce him. . . .
Uh . . . how do you pronounce him . . . ?

THE GLETCHER

See the Gletcher in his cage,
His claws are sharp, his teeth are double.
Thank heaven he's locked up safe inside,
Or we'd all be in terrible trouble!

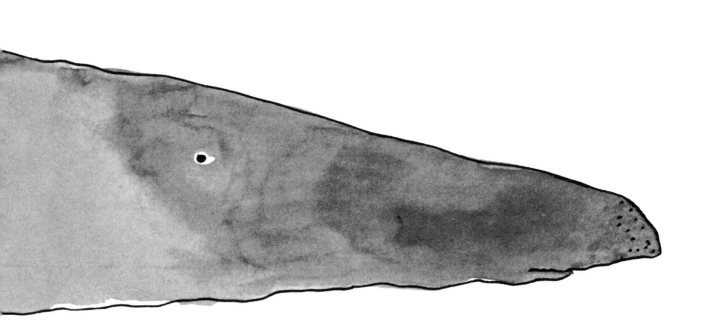

THE TRAP

Let us set a little trap for the Grinch, Grinch, Grinch.
We can catch him if we wait, wait, wait.
I shall be the hunter, and bold, bold, bold,
And you shall be the bait, bait, bait, bait, bait.

THE BIBELY

The Bibely's habits are rather crude
He shuns all ordinary food
And rather enjoys
Girls and boys.
So when you sense him drawing near
Pour some ketchup in your ear
And pretend you're a roast
Or a poached egg on toast
Or a small piece of blueberry pie—
And maybe he'll walk right by.

WHO?

So once again I find some sand in my chicken soup . . .
Now I'm not accusing the Floop
And I don't say that it was the Goppitt,
But whoever it is better stop it . . .
You hear?

WHOEVER IT IS BETTER STOP IT!

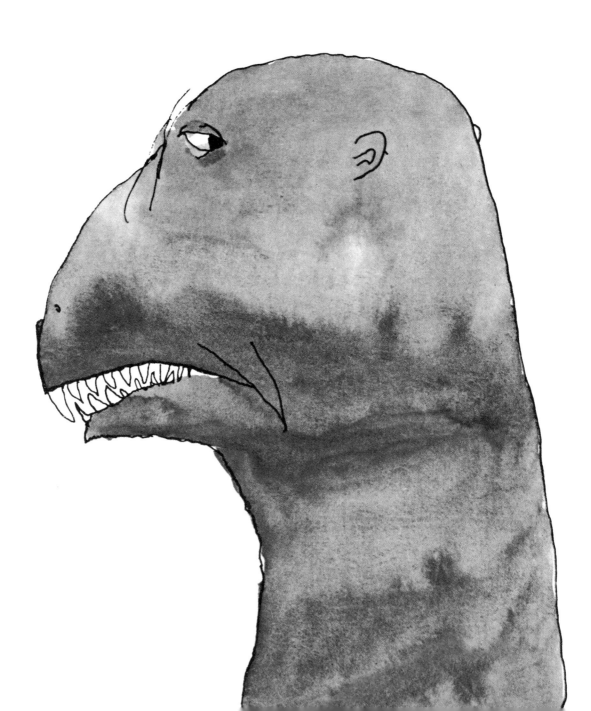

THE
TERRIBLE
FEEZUS

There is a terrible twenty-foot Feezus.
Shhh . . . I don't think he sees us.

SLITHERGADEE

The Slithergadee has crawled out of the sea.
He may catch all the others, but he won't catch me.
No you won't catch me, old Slithergadee,
You may catch all the others, but you wo———

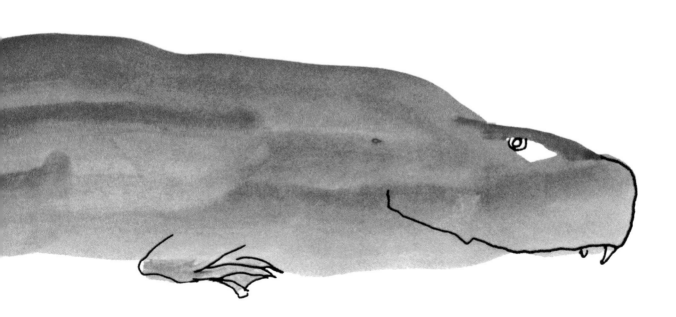

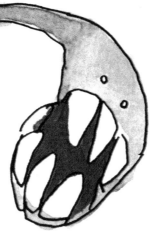

THE WILD GAZITE

Late last night
I'd a terrible fight
With a wild Gazite
With eyes of white
And a fifty-foot height
And he gave me a fright
When he gave me a bite
And then squeezed me so tight.
But I fixed him, alright—
I turned on the light!

POINTY-PEAKED PAVARIUS

The Pointy-Peaked Pavarius,
A creature most gregarious,
Who's never taken serious,
Poor thing.
It doesn't matter where he is,
He's jeered by persons various,
Who shout out, "Lookee, there he is!"
Then wait for him to sing.

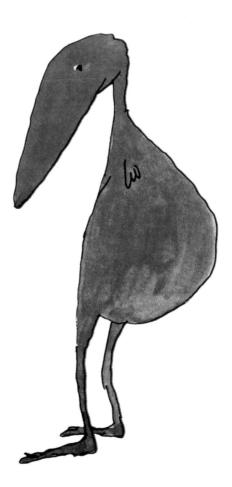

MAN-EATING FULLIT

This is the tail of the
Man-Eating Fullit.
Let's not pull it.

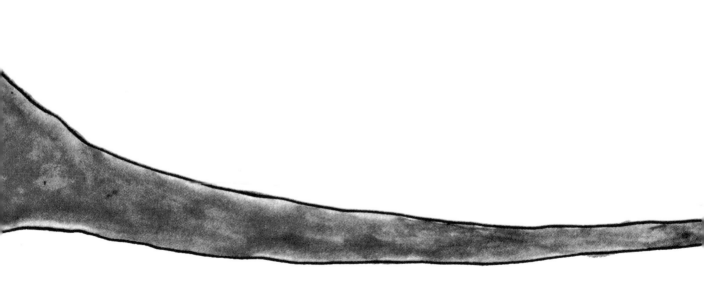

SOMETHING

Something's been eating my mustache again—
I think it's the Skittering Skeep again—
It's gotten to me in my sleep again.

When the Glub-Toothed Sline
Comes to my house to dine,
You may find me in France or Detroit
Or off in Khartoum,
Or in the spare room
Of my Uncle Ed's place in Beloit.

You may call me in Philly,
Racine or Rabat.
You may reach me in Malmö or Ghor.
You may see me in Paris,
And likely as not,
You will run into me at the store.

You may find me in Hamburg,
Or up in St. Paul,
In Kyoto, Kenosha or Nome.
But one thing is sure,
If you find me at all,
You *never* shall find me at home.

GLUB-TOOTHED SLINE

THE GHELI

See the Twenty-Eight-Ton Gheli.
He'd love for you to scratch his belly.

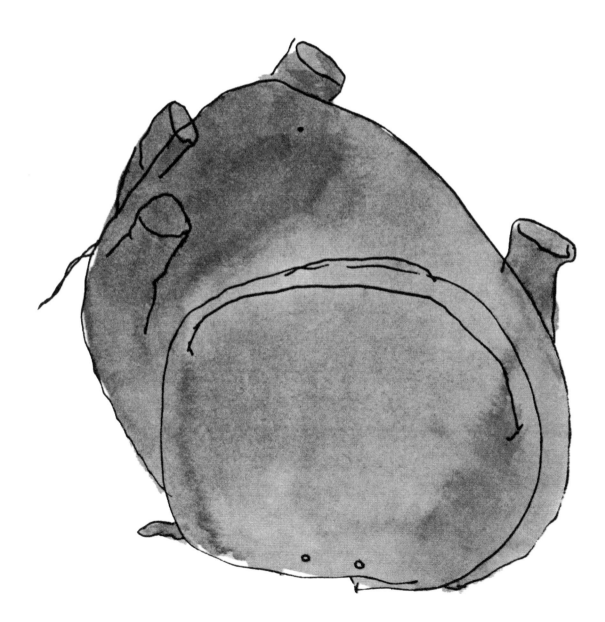

THE SLURM

The Slavery Slurm at the first sign of
trouble will squiver and squimmer and
bend himself double and worgle his elbow
up into his ear and pull in his ankles
and just disappear.

THE
FLUSTERING
PHANT

Some animals pop from cocoons,
While others spring up from the clay.
I've heard that some drop from balloons
Or arrive in some other ridiculous way.
But the Tiny-Toed Flustering Phant
(And please don't repeat that I said it)—
He grows from the stem of the Bibulous plant,
And the snob never lets you forget it.

THE CONSIDERATE
SOFT-SHELLED
PHIZZINT

You'll never know an animal
     more considerate of human feelings
     than the Soft-Shelled Phizzint.
Someone has mistaken this one
     for a pincushion
     and he's too polite to say he isn't.

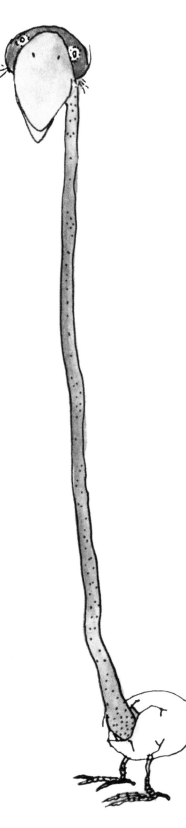

LONG-NECKED PREPOSTEROUS

This is Arnold,
A Long-Necked Preposterous,
Looking around for a female
Long-Necked Preposterous.
But there aren't any.

ABOUT THE BLOATH

In the undergrowth
There dwells the Bloath
Who feeds upon poets and tea.
Luckily I know this about him,
While he knows almost nothing of me.

SEE THE MUFFER

Above, you see the Muffer, who . . .
You don't?
Well anyway, you see his tracks, the Muffer has gone to sup—
You don't?
Why that sly old beast . . .
I do believe he's gone and covered them up!

THE GALLOPING GRISS

Have you seen anything of the Galloping Griss?
Purple-eyed and dripping fat?
If he went that way,
I'll go this.
If he went this way,
I'll go that!

THE GURSDEE

Does anyone here talk Gursdee talk?
Do you know how to say "goodbye"?
For I'd like the Gursdee to leave next Thursday,
And all I can say is "Hi"!

THE PLIGHT OF THE PANADA

In Manitoba, Canada,
There dwells the lop-eared Panada,
A native of Uganada
Who sort of lost his way.

The strangest beast I've ran inta,
He's tended by a janita
Who comes from South Atlanata
Atlanata, G. A.

ONE-LEGGED ZANTZ

Please be kind to the One-Legged Zantz.
Consider his feelings—
Don't ask him to dance.

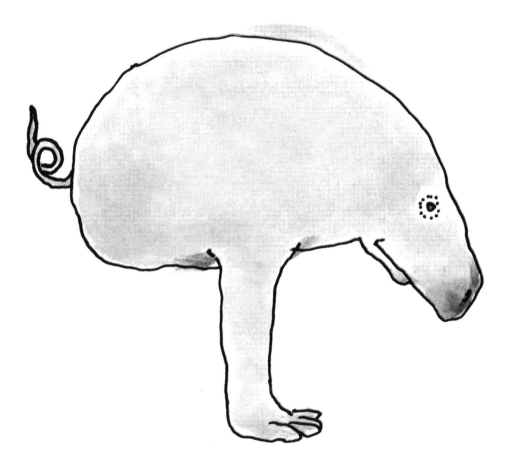

THE FURLESS FLATCHIM

The most contrary beast alive
Is the Furless Flatchim.
What do you think of this clever trap
That I've invented to catch him?

THERE'S A GRITCHEN

There's a Skaverbacked Gritchen
Who lives in my kitchen
And makes his home under the sink.
And he lives upon Gipes
    that crawl out of the pipes
And he takes only Postum to drink.

He is friends with the Lubbard
Who dwells in my cupboard,
And often at night after dark,
They will sit on the stove
    and converse with the Scrove
And catch a few Skinch for a lark.

Then they'll call to the Blaucetts
Who creep from the faucets;
They'll sit on the tea kettle's brim.
And the Slithery Scarbage
    crawl out of the garbage
And jump in the soup for a swim.

IN MY KITCHEN

He'll sing with the Whispies
Who live in Rice Krispies
And serve them my cheese
    and sardines,
And they call to the Zox
    in the old napkin box
To come down and play bridge
    in the beans.

Then he may run a race
To the silverware case
With the Gruppy
    who drinks all my beer,
And he'll dance with the Muvvin
    inside of my oven
And whisper sweet sounds
    in her ear.

For the Gritchen's in love
    with the Muvvin, poor boy,
But *she* loves the Back-Biting Smee—
Or is it the Jase? Well, in any case,
I'm glad you could make it for tea.

A FAMILY AFFAIR

Oh, the Bulbulous Brole
Is a beast with a soul
And a manner serene and sedate.
A model of meekness,
With only one weakness,
And that is for eating his mate.
Heigh-ho,
A masculine need for his mate.

Now the White-Breasted Murd
Is a delicate bird,
With a song that is tenderly sung.
She is gentle and shy,
With a matronly eye,
And a fondness for eating her young.
Heigh-ho,
A motherly love for her young.

The young Gross-Bottomed Grood—
He takes milk for his food
And goopies and bran for his tummy.
And he goos with delight,
When sometime at night,
He can swallow his daddy and mummy.
Heigh-ho,
A filial love fills his tummy.

And, oh, were you here
For the wedding, my dear?
And the quiet buffet that ensued?
When the Bulbulous Brole
Wed the Murd, I am tole,
And produced a young Gross-Bottomed Grood.
Heigh-ho,
A gurgling Gross-Bottomed Grood.

GRU

HOW TO DEAL WITH THE GRU

Don't pooh-pooh the Gru,
For if you do,
He'll bite you through,
And chomp and chew,
And swallow you.
But if you don't,
Don't think he won't.

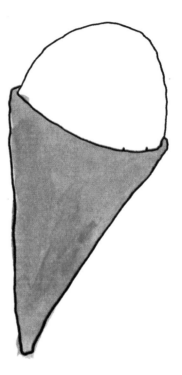

THE BALD-TOP DROAN

I see you there, old Bald-Top Droan
Hiding in that ice-cream cone.
I'll get awful, awful sick
If I give your head a lick.

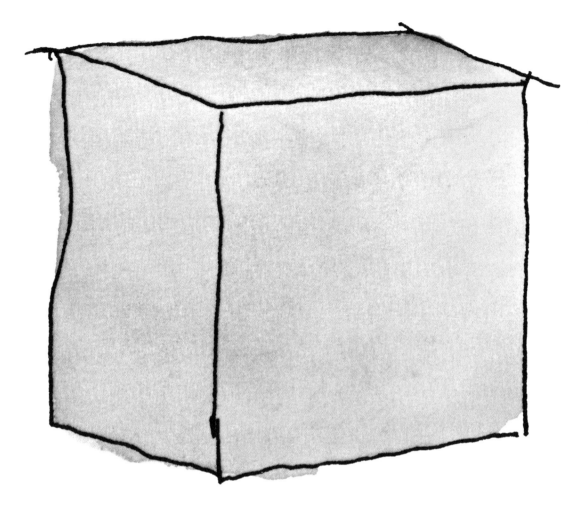

HOW TO CATCH A GLEEECH

If you want to catch a Gleeech,
Take a paper bag
Find a cardboard box
Dig a little hole
Put the bag in the box
Put the box in the hole
Put the Gleeech in the bag
        and there you are.

THE EGG OF THE GREEL

This egg is the Feather-Breasted Greel's.
If it makes you feel funny just looking at it,
Imagine how the *Greel* feels!

THE
SKINNY
ZIPPITY

O pity the poor, poor Zippity,
For he can eat nothing but Greli—
A plant that grows only in New Caledoni,
While the Zippity lives in New Delhi.

OOPS!

We've been caught by a Quick-Digesting Gink
And now we are dodging his teeth
And now we are restin'
In his small intestine,
And now we're back out on the street. . . .

THE ZUMBIES

The Ostrich is known to bury his head.
The Zumby, so much more discreetly,
At the very first inkling of danger or dread,
Will bury himself most completely.

If he glimpses the sound or the odor of man,
He envisions a horrible death,
So he burrows himself deep down into the sand,
And sits there, just holding his breath.

So the next time you're down to the beach at the strand,
So sunny and splashy and gay,
Remember, the Zumbies sit under the sand,
Just waiting for you to go 'way.

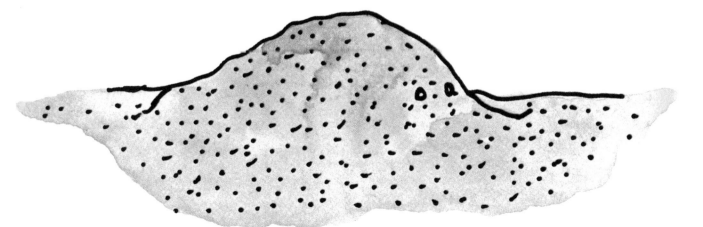

THE FLYING FESTOON

I am going to ride on the Flying Festoon,
I'll jump on his back and I'll whistle a tune,
And we'll fly to the outermost tip of the moon,
The Flying Festoon and I.

Oh, I'm taking some crackers, a ball and a prune,
And we're leaving this evening precisely at noon,
For I'm going to fly with the Flying Festoon,
Just as soon as he learns how to fly.

IN WAUKESHA WISC.

In Waukesha Wisc.
You take quite a risk
Whenever you go to the movies,
For there in the dark lurks the Double-Toed Vaark
And the man-eating Scale-Faced Scoovies.

There are Gobble-Eyed Gohrks
And Slimy-Tailed Borks
And Hunchlings, and Broggy-Beaked Byzes
And Gumboons and Grobs and Globamabobs
And Creelzies of various sizes.

There are Bony-Backed Bleaks
And Razor-Toothed Kleeks
And Wailees and Glumpaching Gorkle,
And the shivery shrieks from the Gaitering Geeks
Are worse than the snort of the Snorkle.

There are Glumgurds and Speem,
And the Grizimy's scream
May awaken the Foul-Tempered Fisk
And the Scale-Faced Scoovies that dwell in the movies
Right here in Waukesha Wisc.

GUMPLEGUTCH

Go over and play with the Gumplegutch, Tommy,
The Gumplegutch loves to play.
You may bounce on his belly
And call him old Nelly
And fill up his nostrils with clay.
Don't be 'fraid of his fangs
Or that one yellow eye
Or the scales on his tail, my dear.
Go over and play with the Gumplegutch, Tommy,
There's nothing at all to fear.

I'll wait for you here.

THE WILD CHEROTE

I'd like a coat of Wild Cherote.
It's warm and fleecy as can be.
But note: What if the Wild Cherote
Would like a coat of Me?

THE FRIENDLY OLD
SLEEPY-EYED SKURK

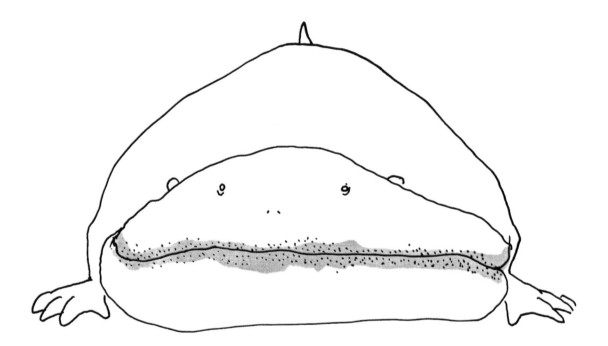

The Sleepy-Eyed Skurk, he's a nice old thing.
He'll let you sit inside his mouth.
If you knock on his chin,
He'll let you in.
But I rather doubt
He'll let you out.

SQUISHY SQUASHY STAGGITALL

When
Singing songs of
Scaryness,
Of bloodyness
And hairyness,
I-feel-obligated-at-this-moment-to-remind-you
Of-the-most-ferocious-beast-of-all,
Six thousand tons,
And nine miles tall,
The Squishy Squashy Staggitall . . .
That's standing right behind you.

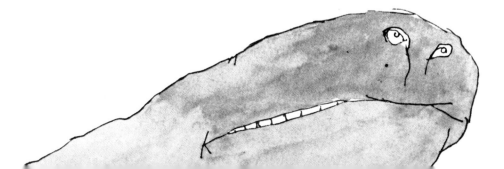